★★★AMERICAN ACHIEVEMENTS★★★

THE BEAT OF A NATION

HOW HIP-HOP SHAPED AMERICAN CULTURE AND INSPIRED THE WORLD

DR. MONICA B. MORALL-BAKER

Lerner Publications ◆ Minneapolis

For Mom and Dad, and to Dwight, my love. Special thanks to Lyle LeDuff for your inspiration and expertise.

Lerner Publications Company
An imprint of Lerner Publishing Group, Inc.
241 First Avenue North
Minneapolis, MN 55401 USA

For reading levels and more information, look up this title at www.lernerbooks.com.

Main body text set in Aptifer Slab LT Pro. Typeface provided by Linotype AG.

Photo Editor: Giliane Mansfeldt

Library of Congress Cataloging-in-Publication Data

Names: Morall-Baker, Monica B., author.
Title: The beat of a nation : how hip-hop shaped American culture and inspired the world / Dr. Monica B. Morall-Baker.
Description: Minneapolis : Lerner Publications, 2026. | Series: American achievements | Includes bibliographical references and index. | Audience: Ages 8–12 | Audience: Grades 4–6 | Summary: "Hip-hop is a cultural movement that began in New York City in the 1970s. Young readers discover the beginnings of hip-hop, how it evolved and spread globally over time, and its lasting impact"— Provided by publisher.
Identifiers: LCCN 2025013218 (print) | LCCN 2025013219 (ebook) | ISBN 9798765688861 (library binding) | ISBN 9798348028718 (paperback) | ISBN 9798765695623 (epub)
Subjects: LCSH: Rap (Music)—History and criticism—Juvenile literature. | Hip-hop—Juvenile literature. | Rap (Music)—Social aspects—Juvenile literature.
Classification: LCC ML3531 .M6614 2026 (print) | LCC ML3531 (ebook) | DDC 782.421649—dc23/eng/20250326

LC record available at https://lccn.loc.gov/2025013218
LC ebook record available at https://lccn.loc.gov/2025013219

Manufactured in the United States of America
1-1012623-54716-6/26/2025

TABLE OF CONTENTS

CHAPTER 1

A NEW MUSIC GENRE

Actor and rapper 2 Chainz performs during *A Grammy Salute to 50 Years of Hip-Hop* in 2023.

In 2023 people all over the world tuned in to watch the concert special *A Grammy Salute to 50 Years of Hip-Hop*. Big Daddy Kane, Doug E. Fresh, MC Lyte, and other rappers performed their biggest hits. Newer artists such as Latto and GloRilla brought fresh performances to the stage.

The artists shared the stage to celebrate the past fifty years of hip-hop and to honor the impact hip-hop culture has had on music and the world. When hip-hop music began, many people thought that it would only be popular for a short time. But over fifty years later, it is still one of the most popular genres of music.

Rapper and producer Jermaine Dupri onstage during *A Grammy Salute to 50 Years of Hip-Hop*

THE START OF HIP-HOP

Hip-hop music started in the early 1970s in the Black and Latinx communities in New York City. Clive Campbell, better known as DJ Kool Herc, and his sister Cindy Campbell held a back-to-school party in the Bronx. Rumor has it that DJ Kool Herc played an extended version of the instrumental part of the records so that people could dance longer through the break in the lyrics. This experiment was a success, and hip-hop music was born.

DJ Kool Herc DJing in 2000

Grandmaster Flash was one of the first DJs who tried scratching.

Young people from all over New York went to parties to hear this new style of music. Disc jockeys, or DJs, played records on two turntables. This allowed them to mix the songs together. DJs also acted as a master of ceremonies, or MC (emcee). They talked in between the songs to hype the crowd.

Grand Wizzard Theodore, Grandmaster Flash, and other DJs tried scratching. They pushed the record back and forth as the music played to make a scratching sound. They also rhymed or rapped over the beats.

Griots in Burkina Faso, a country in West Africa, use poetry and music to tell family histories.

THE ROOTS

Hip-hop music has its roots in African, Jamaican, Latinx, and Black American culture. The West African griot culture inspired rhyming and storytelling, which is part of rap. In Jamaica in the 1960s, DJs yelled at the audience to get them to dance. This was called toasting.

People in Black American communities exchanged humorous insults in a game called the dozens. This game turned into rap battles. During these battles, rappers face off to see who has the best lyrics and flow.

Black churches also influenced rapping. Preachers often call out phrases, and the members of the church respond. This call-and-response technique is used to connect with church members.

Hip-hop artists often blend different music genres. Hip-hop music has blended with disco and funk. It has also blended with rhythm and blues (R&B), soul, and more genres.

Rappers performing at an event in Spain in 2021

HITMAKERS

Many artists and hit songs helped hip-hop become popular. In 1979 the Sugarhill Gang released "Rapper's Delight." This song reached number 36 on *Billboard* Hot 100—a chart of the week's most popular songs. It also reached a global audience.

MC Sha-Rock was part of the hip-hop group Funky 4 + 1. She was the first female emcee of a rap group. MC Sha-Rock became known for her rhyming style. In 1984 fourteen-year-old Roxanne Shanté released her hit, "Roxanne's Revenge." She wrote this diss song in response to rap group UTFO's hit "Roxanne, Roxanne."

The Sugarhill Gang reached a global audience through their music.

Record labels are music companies that sign, manage, and promote artists. In 1984 Russell Simmons and Rick Rubin founded Def Jam Recordings. The label has worked with major rap stars such as Public Enemy and LL Cool J. Def Jam has shaped hip-hop culture around the world through its influence on music, film, and fashion.

THE MOTHER OF HIP-HOP

In the 1970s, singer Sylvia Robinson cofounded Sugar Hill Records. It was one of the first hip-hop record labels. Robinson became known as the Mother of Hip-Hop because she was the producer of two of the biggest early hip-hop records: "Rapper's Delight" by the Sugarhill Gang and "The Message" by Grandmaster Flash and the Furious Five.

The Mother of Hip-Hop, Sylvia Robinson, in 1973

Rihanna takes the stage while touring in 2016.

In 1996 producer and rapper Dr. Dre formed the record label Aftermath Entertainment. He signed several successful artists, including Eminem and 50 Cent. In 2008 rapper Jay-Z founded the entertainment company Roc Nation. The company has worked with Rihanna, Megan Thee Stallion, Big Sean, and other artists.

Some record labels focus on creativity and allow their artists to have more control over their music. Quality Control Music has worked with hip-hop artists such as Migos and City Girls. Generation Now has worked with artists such as Killumantii, Luh Tyler, Lil Uzi Vert, and Jack Harlow.

FIRST BILLIONAIRE RAPPER

In 2019 *Forbes* magazine named Jay-Z the first billionaire rapper. He made money from his music and other businesses. He owned a clothing label, a music streaming service, and a sports agency. Since 2019 his entertainment company Roc Nation has partnered with the National Football League to help create the Super Bowl halftime shows.

Jay-Z attends the Grammy Awards in 2025.

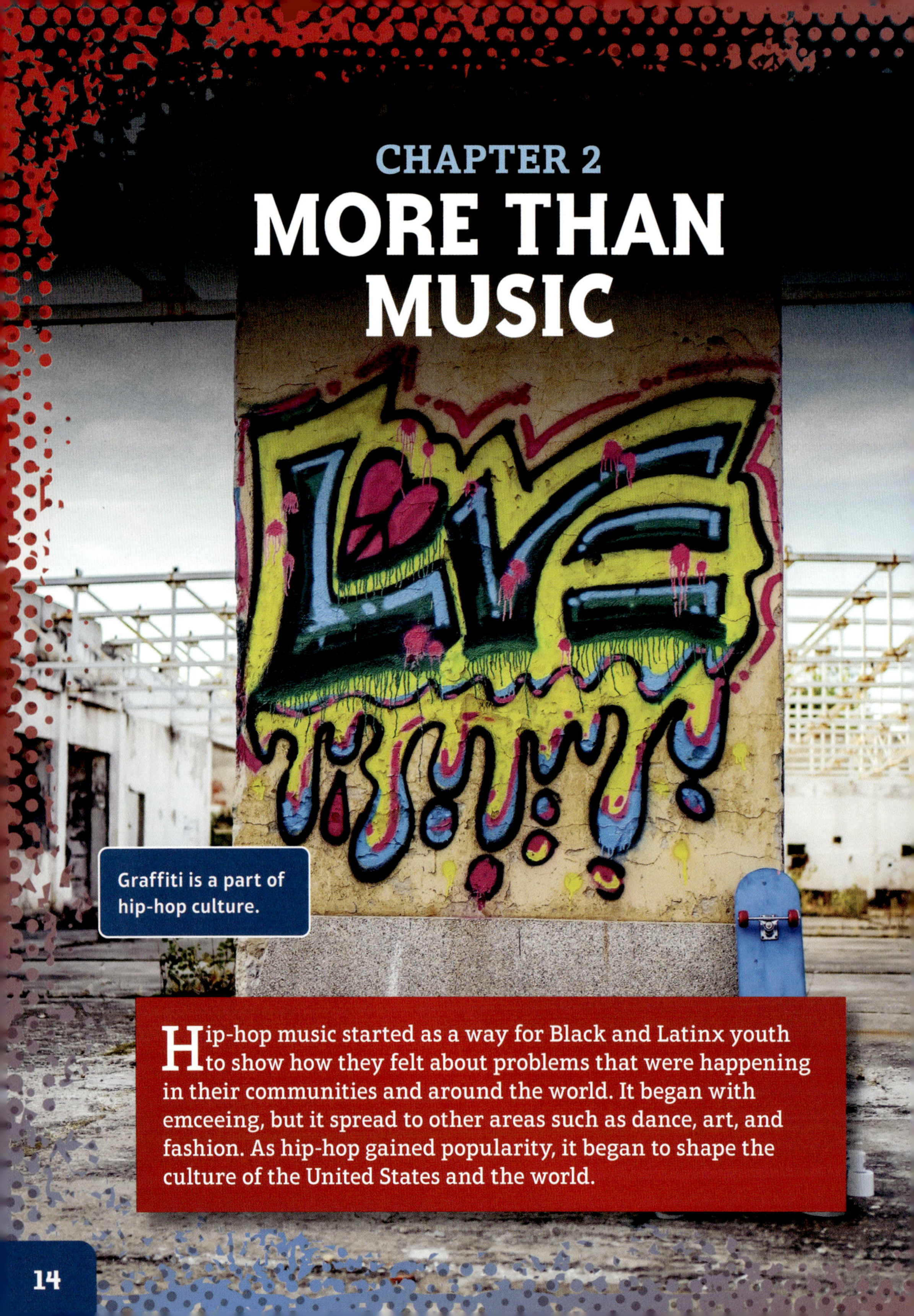

CHAPTER 2

MORE THAN MUSIC

Graffiti is a part of hip-hop culture.

Hip-hop music started as a way for Black and Latinx youth to show how they felt about problems that were happening in their communities and around the world. It began with emceeing, but it spread to other areas such as dance, art, and fashion. As hip-hop gained popularity, it began to shape the culture of the United States and the world.

BREAKING, GRAFFITI, AND FASHION

Breakdancing, or breaking, is a style of dance. It includes footwork and tricks. Dancers of this style are known as breakdancers, breakers, or B-boys and B-girls. Breakers dance during the "break" in the music. This is when the vocals and instruments stop so that only the drums are playing.

B-girl Toquinha competes at an event in 2024.

Breaking began in the Bronx in the 1970s and changed and grew over time. The Rock Steady Crew became one of the first popular breaking groups. Breakers perform all over the world. In 2024 breaking was an event at the Olympics in Paris, France.

Graffiti is a form of art. Graffiti artists often write or draw on walls, subway cars, and other public surfaces without permission. Artists use graffiti to express how they think or feel about something going on in the world.

HIP-HOP MEETS ART

Artist Jean-Michel Basquiat (*left*) began his career as a graffiti artist in the 1970s. He became known all over the world. He influenced hip-hop culture and inspired other hip-hop artists. Kendrick Lamar and other rappers have mentioned Basquiat in their songs. In 2013 Jay-Z bought Basquiat's painting *Mecca* for $4.5 million.

Rapper Heavy D (*left*) and DJ Jam Master Jay attend the 1991 Soul Train Music Awards.

Fashion is another way for youth to express themselves. Both breaking and graffiti have influenced hip-hop fashion. Hip-hop clothing often features graffiti elements such as bright colors and cool sayings or designs. Breakers often wear baggy clothes that allow them to move freely. Their style became part of everyday streetwear, a style that represents the culture of urban youth.

CHAPTER 3

THE REVOLUTION

Civil rights activist Martin Luther King Jr. addresses a crowd in 1965.

Many people fought for racial equality during the Civil Rights Movement in the 1950s and 1960s. Music played a large role. Anthems such as "We Shall Overcome" inspired people and brought attention to the cause. Hip-hop artists of the past and present have also used music to talk about racial equality and other issues. Many people view hip-hop as the music of revolution.

Grandmaster Flash and the Furious Five's 1982 song "The Message" talked about the economic issues and violence that the Black community faced. In the late 1980s, KRS-One founded the Stop the Violence Movement. He produced the song "Self Destruction." MC Lyte, Ms. Melodie, Public Enemy, and many other artists worked on the song that spoke against violence.

Grandmaster Flash and the Furious Five in 1982

The 1990 song "We're All in the Same Gang" also brought artists together to speak against violence. Artists such as Ice-T, Ice Cube, and Snoop Dogg have also rapped about police brutality and unequal economic opportunities for Black people. Sister Souljah spoke out against issues such as racism.

Some artists have written and performed songs to uplift the Black community. Tupac Shakur's songs empowered Black youth and influenced other artists, including Kendrick Lamar. Ms. Melodie

Tupac Shakur perfoms at the Paramount Theater in New York City in 1994.

Monie Love (*left*) and Queen Latifah singing "Ladies First" in 1990

wrote songs that highlighted the strength of women. In 1989 Queen Latifah and Monie Love created the women's anthem "Ladies First." In 1993 Queen Latifah's song "U.N.I.T.Y." promoted unity and respect for women.

ONGOING FIGHT FOR CHANGE

The hip-hop community continues to influence politics and current issues. After Kendrick Lamar's song "Alright" was released in 2015, it became an anthem for the Black Lives Matter movement. His song united people as they marched during this movement to protest police brutality. In 2016 President Barack Obama invited artists such as Ludacris, Chance the Rapper, and Nicki Minaj to the White House to talk about problems with the criminal justice system and other issues.

Protesters march at a 2025 rally in Los Angeles, California.

Megan Thee Stallion takes the stage in 2020.

In 2020 police officers killed George Floyd, an unarmed Black man in Minnesota, and Breonna Taylor, an unarmed Black woman in Kentucky. After these killings, Megan Thee Stallion and Cardi B spoke out against police brutality. Both artists also use social media to encourage people to vote so that their voices can be heard.

Queen Latifah and Newark, New Jersey, Mayor Ras Baraka attend an event for a housing project in 2022.

Many rappers such as Killer Mike and T.I. create businesses that help support Black, Latinx, and other underrepresented communities. Newark, New Jersey, Mayor Ras Baraka partnered with Queen Latifah in 2022. They held an event to promote community and nonviolence. They also worked on a housing project.

Rappers in other countries relate to the struggle for equality and freedom. Since the Russian invasion of Ukraine in 2022, hip-hop music has grown in popularity in Russia. But Russian hip-hop artists face danger because of their criticism of Russian President Vladimir Putin.

MAJOR PERFORMANCE

Kendrick Lamar's 2025 Super Bowl halftime show was an important moment in hip-hop. His show explored themes of American history and Black identity. Many people viewed his performance as a message of strength for Black people. Lamar's show had the most viewers of any Super Bowl halftime show. Over 133 million people watched it.

Kendrick Lamar performing during his 2025 Super Bowl halftime show

LOOKING ONWARD

Hip-hop is one of the most popular genres of music in the United States. Hip-hop music makes over $15 billion every year. Technology is changing how artists create and share music. Artists can use artificial intelligence and other digital tools to create beats and change sounds and voices. Streaming services such as SoundCloud let fans listen to music from all over the world at any time.

Producer Metro Boomin onstage in 2024

Rapper Doechii presents an award at the 2025 iHeartRadio Music Awards.

Hip-hop's influence extends far beyond music. Hip-hop culture presents a message of unity for everyone in the United States and around the world.

HIP-HOP TIMELINE

★ **1973** Hip-hop begins in the Black and Latinx communities in the Bronx, New York City.

★ **1979** The Sugarhill Gang releases "Rapper's Delight."

Sylvia Robinson cofounds the record label Sugar Hill Records.

★ **1982** Grandmaster Flash and the Furious Five release "The Message."

★ **1989** Queen Latifah and Monie Love release "Ladies First," which becomes a women's anthem.

★ **1996** Dr. Dre creates the record label Aftermath Entertainment.

★ **2008** Jay-Z creates the entertainment company Roc Nation.

★ **2015** Kendrick Lamar releases "Alright," which becomes an anthem for the Black Lives Matter movement.

★ **2023** Hip-hop artists and fans celebrate the fiftieth anniversary of hip-hop.

★ **2024** Breakers from around the world compete at the Olympics in Paris, France.

★ **2025** Kendrick Lamar performs the most viewed Super Bowl halftime show in history.

GLOSSARY

anthem: a song that is used as a symbol for a group or movement

criminal justice system: a system of people such as law enforcement and court officials who ensure public safety and rule on people who are accused of crimes

economic: having to do with the money system

empower: to give power to

equality: the state of being equal in rights and opportunities

genre: a category of art, such as music or literature, that is characterized by a particular style

griot: an oral storyteller, especially in parts of West Africa

influence: the power to affect or change

police brutality: the overuse of force by a police officer

producer: a person who helps guide the creation of music

turntable: a rotating platform that plays records

LEARN MORE

Britannica Kids: Hip-Hop
https://kids.britannica.com/kids/article/hip-hop/399968

Clark, Trey. *Cardi B*. Creative Education and Creative Paperbacks, 2026.

The Hip Hop Museum
https://thhm.org

Kiddle: Kendrick Lamar Facts for Kids
https://kids.kiddle.co/Kendrick_Lamar

Kiddle: Roxanne Shanté Facts for Kids
https://kids.kiddle.co/Roxanne_Shante

Lilley, Matt. *Hip-Hop*. Focus Readers, 2025.

Morall-Baker, Dr. Monica B. *Hip-Hop and Social Justice: Rhymes of Resistance*. Lerner Publications, 2026.

Shepherd, Crown. *Hip-Hop Music: Songs That Changed the World*. Lerner Publications, 2026.

INDEX

PHOTO ACKNOWLEDGMENTS

Image credits: Frazer Harrison/Getty Images for The Recording Academy, pp. 4, 5; Henry Iddon/PYMCA/Avalon/Getty Images, p. 6; David Corio/Michael Ochs Archives/Getty Images, p. 7; Irene Abdou/Alamy, p. 8; Aldara Zarraoa/Getty Images, p. 9; Michael Ochs Archive/Getty Images, p. 10; Don Paulsen/Michael Ochs Archives/Getty Images, p. 11; Francesco Castaldo\Archivio Francesco Castaldo\Mondadori/Getty Images, p. 12; Kevin Mazur/Getty Images, p. 13; LordHenriVoton/Getty Images, p. 14; Dean Treml/Red Bull/Getty Images, p. 15; Rose Hartman/Getty Images, p. 16; Vinnie Zuffante/Getty Images, p. 17; Alan Raia/Newsday/Getty Images, p. 18; SR Agency/Gentle Look/Getty Images, p. 19; Al Pereira/Michael Ochs Archives/Getty Images, pp. 20, 21; eleuk Acar/Anadolu/Getty Images, p. 22; Rich Fury/Getty Images, p. 23; Bennett Raglin/Getty Images, p. 24; Jamie Squire/Getty Images, p. 25; Prince Williams/WireImage/Getty Images, p. 26; Kevin Winter/Getty Images, p. 27. Design elements: Sanches11/Shutterstock; Mooam/Shutterstock; brwen/Shutterstock. Cover: AP Photo/Michael Owens.